American Poetry Pure & Simple

Dolly M. Gorham

AuthorHouse™
1663 Liberty Drive
Bloomington, IN 47403
www.authorhouse.com
Phone: 1-800-839-8640

© 2011 Dolly M. Gorham. All rights reserved.

No part of this book may be reproduced, stored in a retrieval system, or transmitted by any means without the written permission of the author.

First published by AuthorHouse   5/23/2011

ISBN: 978-1-4567-4899-9 (e)
ISBN: 978-1-4567-4900-2 (hc)
ISBN: 978-1-4567-4901-9 (sc)

Library of Congress Control Number: 2011903914

Printed in the United States of America

Any people or scenes depicted in imagery are provided, with express written permission, by the author, Dolly M. Gorham, and such images are being used for illustration purposes only. All imagery © Dolly M. Gorham.

This book is printed on acid-free paper.

Because of the dynamic nature of the Internet, any web addresses or links contained in this book may have changed since publication and may no longer be valid. The views expressed in this work are solely those of the author and do not necessarily reflect the views of the publisher, and the publisher hereby disclaims any responsibility for them.

Preface

I'm writing this book of poems because those who have crossed my path have urged me to create this collection. They told me that my writing is pure & simple; thus, the title. Also they have said that my writing shows a true heart & a feel for America.

I hope you all enjoy!

It has been fun creating this book. The only thing that could make it better, for me, is that others may enjoy the poems & meanings as much as I did compiling them

I would love to have you share any of your thoughts about the poems with me.

Email: Dolly@importantaccessories.com
Subject: American Poetry Pure & Simple

Acknowledgement

I would like to thank both of my awesome children, Eric Turner & Leah (Turner) Morisi, as well as my sisters & brothers. I'd like to thank Christina Lawrence, Belinda Lawrence, Lisa Brennan & Samantha Beal who are all dear to my heart. They listened, read, & put up with the ranting of a crazy woman.

I love all of you!

An honorable mention needs to go to a few more good people: Ali Vargas; Holly Larsen; Ron Bufton II; Gene Petry; Mark Kaleta; Rick Kirkland; Don Porter & Rob Midgley.

Thanks for all of your kind words!

My children, grandchildren & grand-dog (Busta), are my inspirations of love.

Contents

Preface vii

Acknowledgement ix

Change in Time 1
Money Doesn't Make Our Life Happy It Just Makes It Easier 3
Touched 5
Our Country's Land 7
A Father; A Veteran of War 8
The Day I Met My Father 11
The Man You Are 13
The Eyes of a Child 15
Speak Kindly 17
A Heart 19
Grandma's Inspiration 21
Friends 23
A New Girl in Town 25
Easter 27
Halloween 29
An American Holiday "Thanksgiving" 31
Christmas 33
Merry Christmas 35
New Year 37
The Color of My Skin 39
Our Mother 41
Mother 43
Marriage 45
Sisters 47
Think Positive 49
A Conversation 51
Divorce 53
Chocolate 55
Patience 57
Tradition 59
Autism 61
Death 63
Life 65
Lines for an Airplane Ride 66
In-Law 69
Internet Dating 71
If You "Are" What You Eat 73

About the Author 75

Change in Time

Our roles change as the times pass
  No idea so many titles would appear
Maybe starting out as a small girl from Mass
  Ending as a grandma in a state no where near

A daughter, a sister, an auntie, that's not all
  A mom, a grandma & a wife
Never realizing how temporary; these titles would fall
  Losing titles is just part of life

It's like a clock with its hands as they constantly pass
  Tick tock as the time & minutes go by
The clock's face is one that never wrinkles; Alas!
  Unlike most humans' that wrinkle; Oh my!

Unprepared how we are to the change in time
  Our gears constantly change in speed
The gears tend to slow with a life so sublime
  Then speed up for a change or a need

Time stops for no-one as an old poet said
  So true toward the change in time
Since we are out of control & then maybe dead
  Love life; smile always; it's never a crime

Money Doesn't Make Our Life Happy It Just Makes It Easier

Money runs our lives as we let it
   We can choose this path each day
Just as the sun rises or the candle is lit
   Our paths will continue as it may

This continues until we start to wake
   To the realization of a life so sleazy
Money can't make us happy; that's fake
   It only makes our material life easy

Once we start down a new path with less money
   We start to see that there is much we don't need
So use GPS & continue alone or with a honey
   We will experience a new life; just plant the seed

So we cut our cards & our own hair
   Eat at home & drink less famous coffee
Just a few more things to cut as we fare
   Our new path; a new life; let's be free

If all could understand, it's not a unique path
   Just one that is spiritual & so full
No one would be sad; burdened; or feel wrath
   It's just a new path; enjoy; feel the pull

Touched

People look differently at the meaning of "Touched"
    Is it a tangible hold; Feel with fingers; Clutched?
It means so much more to me than just that
    It is to be moved, perceived or come into contact

It can be physical or spiritual; Depending on the view
    It can be to hug, hold hands or just to stand by you
The spiritual is faceted & more in depth by far
    It affects each differently, no matter who you are

Any meaning of "Touched" can feel so true
    A book, song or look, it's all about you
It travels through time for all eternity
    Staying stagnant or moving on to the next city

I pray each day that more humans will try
    To touch, be touched so their hearts will fly
Anyone can start this small, but great, endeavor
    Their energy; their spirit; Will live on forever

Our Country's Land

Our country's land changes as we build an overpass
  No idea so many houses or roads would appear
At first a rural place with vastness over the pass
  Now a metropolitan area; Animals must fear

A cow, bull, buck, & buffalo; that's not all
  Mooing & grazing should be a scene in our life
Never realizing how temporary; the hills will all fall
  Losing vastness is part of our country's land strife

May it be sheep, horses or cows, they all feel the lash
  Herded down streets as cars pass with their haze
The animal's fate is controlled by man's need for cash
  They are the road-kill of the roads as they blaze

Unprepared for the change in our country's land
  The speed of change heeds to our country's lead
The movements of the animals disappear with sand
  But linger by untouched rivers; woods; pasture to feed

Change stops for no animal as the politics tread
  So true toward the change of our country's land
Since we are not in control & pretty much just led
  Change this; Protect life; Speak-out; Lend a hand!

A Father; A Veteran of War

It's Father's Day without "Dad"; maybe nine or ten
   He's remembered by who & what he's been
He has been gone & missed for quite a few years
   He was a great man who deserves many cheers

Born in the early part of the nineteenth century
   The "Great Depression" was arriving with its fury
His parents were born in the late eighteen century
   One of twelve children with futures a bit blurry

Charles Kenneth Gorham was the name all knew
   He was known as "Kenny" to most; "Charlie" by few
His name given by Milton H. & Grace (Bond) Gorham
   What title he was called, depended on what forum

He was born November 1st, 1922; on "All Saint's Day"
   His date of birth reflects his heart most will say
Born in a house, which today does not exist
   Full of honesty; valor; one not to raise a fist

His young days were silly; rambunctious with others
   He was a daredevil. Not as much as his brothers
Riding motor scooters down hills without any hands
   Joining the CCC's; off to work government lands

The CCC's, called the Civilian Conservation Core
   He wished all of his kids had a chance to serve for
A time & a job that he was just so proud of
   An experience he talked about with great love

<u>(Continued on next page)</u>

A Father; A Veteran of War (Continued)

He was a cute young man with not enough weight
    He ate & was healthy but to be thin was his fate
In order to meet the weight required by the core
    That day he drank water; more water; then more

He served the Navy, with brothers & best friend
    World War II broke out; worried how it would end
His brothers & friend, sent on ships to distant places
    His letters eased his & his friend's mom's faces

His ship pulled out of "Pearl Harbor" just days before
    Struggled to find out if anyone he knew was ashore
The island & people were demolished by bombs
    Devastation; His letters helped update the moms

His brothers & friend all made it back to shore
    Then home to their little town; all veterans of war
Instilled in his kids, remember wars & their reasons
    His memory will live on; today & through all seasons

The Day I Met My Father

Today I wake & I am thirty-seven
   I am a woman, a mother, & a wife
My path to this point was not always heaven
   But now, it is my choice, my pleasure & my life

My roles to this point are colorful, I'll say
   Experiencing happiness, sadness; Oh, some drama
Somewhat living in a reality show or a play
   Always surrounded by love, the lord & my mamma

This day is so special beyond any whim
   I've dreamed of this day for so long
In my mind there was always a thought of "Him"
   That "Him" whom I would want to belong

I hope my "Him" really feels the same
   A "Him" that I can call "DAD"
A "DAD" who I can hug & bring to life with a name
   A father, a man; One I really wanted to know I had

Pinch me! Pinch me! I'm not sure how to feel
   First a hug, maybe tears, & questions, is he mine?
A real dad is arriving into my life today
   I know the lord will make this day just fine

The Man You Are

Just a boy from my graduating class
    Not young, with time continuing to pass
He is true to himself. He inspires me
    He is one of a kind. You must agree

One of three boys in a great family tree
    He's the replica of his father, you will see
A Harley rider & country boy to the core
    A heart that is good & kind; Trust that for sure

He makes his momma proud; He's good
    He treats a woman the way he should
Time has passed, since our paths crossed
    He's a dad & a grandpa; nothing glossed

Once a boy; Now a man; Not much has changed
    A bit gray with girth; not one to be exchanged
He is always a true friend & cares about life
    He has endured more than his share of strife

Not much to be said about this country boy
    What you see is what you get; He's not coy
Be proud when he considers you to be good
    It's a title that matters & one that should

He keeps a lot to himself; Sharing with only a few
    You can try to infiltrate, but he must choose you
He may live near, but from me it is far
    Pay homage & embrace, "The Man You Are"

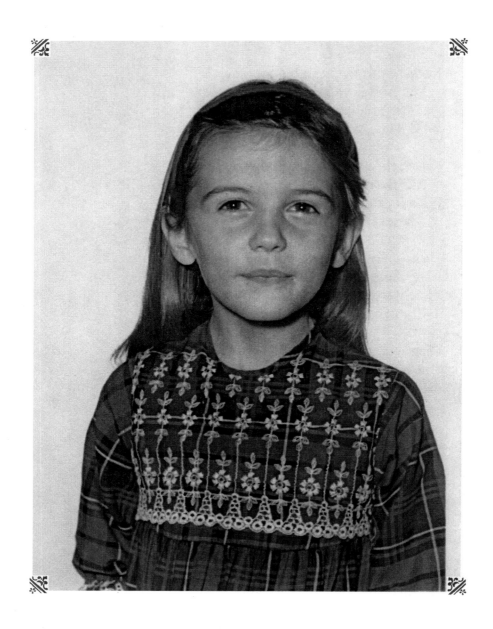

The Eyes of a Child

Look into the eyes of a child not misled
    So beautiful & innocent for sure
Untainted by the new world that's ahead
    Not knowing what will be in store

Eyes big with joy; sometimes wet with tears
    Little things seem quite immense during this time
Who can fathom that we went through those years
    Little things for us now; maybe just a twist of lime

Eyes look to Moms & Dads; their leaders; no vote
    Brothers & sisters, protectors, peers, & guides
Can we remember any thoughts; even a small note
    Want for a child's eye with the changing of tides

Each day, year or century; the eyes see much
    Who can possibly predict; Happiness; Joy; Pain
Eyes of a determinist or randomnist may try such
    That type of prediction is done with naught gain

"If I knew back then what I know now"; Nope
    Change would happen to our life & mate
Pandora's Box was left for all eyes to see; Hope
    The key back to the eyes of a child; Faith; Fate

Speak Kindly

Speak kindly your words
   As unkind words may hurt
Unkind words that are said
   Are unkind, mean & curt

Speak kindly your words
   As the same message is sent
Unkind words that are said
   Show an unkind sentiment

Speak kindly your words
   Your actions speak louder
Unkind words that are said
   Can't make you feel prouder

Speak kindly your words
   As your spirit shows through
Unkind words that are said
   May just reflect upon you

A Heart

A heart can be true
   If you lead it that way
It is only "You"
   That can have that say

A heart can be pure
   If you chose that way
It is only "You" for sure
   That can; doth pray

A Heart can be blue
   If you let it be that way
It is only "You"
   That lets come what may

A heart is what makes you
   If you want it that way
It is only "You"
   That makes you Okay

Grandma's Inspiration

You grow in grandma's garden like a flower
    All I know is what I see
You are my grandson & with love I'll shower
    To keep that smile on your face around me

The rays from the sun
    How bright & full of warmth they are
Match the energy from your fun
    Which shines & brightens near & far

The sparkle from the indigo stars above
    How bright they really can shine
Match the sparkle in your eyes full of love
    They are bright blue, so true, & fine

How special you are beyond my wish
    Starting out so small, growing smart & fast
You giggle, smile, & wiggle like a fish
    With your heart, you make each day such a blast

You communicate with sign language; sounds; motion
    You say, "Grandma" with a huge growl & a smile
So cute; offering hugs; smiles; kisses with a potion
    With you it's guaranteed love forever & a while

You are my dear, precious grandson
    One who I truly, truly just love
You are so special to me & so fun
    My own dancing star from above

Friends

A buddy; best friend; mate
    A person whom you can be free
An acquaintance; co-worker; comrade
    A person to share a coffee

An ally; pen pal; internet friend
    A person who shares special ties
A confidant; blood brother; BFF
    A person who cares; no lies

A girlfriend; wife; mother
    A person to share life's goals
A boyfriend; husband; father
    A person to raise a toast; Skoal!

All are friends of different levels
    All are friends of different shades
All make a life, each day, worth while
    All meant to cross our path; no evades

A New Girl in Town

She is the new girl in town
   Beautiful; smiling; no frown
She has smiling Irish blue eyes
   She brightens up our lives

She keeps her mom on her toes
   With her beginning eating woes
She's a "Daddy's" girl
   With flickering eyes a whirl

She wants to run with her brother
   But is satisfied snuggling with mother
She's here to live in this world
   Loves grandma; to be twirled

She is the queen of the roost
   Her personality; quite a boost
She is such a happy child
   Who tends to get a little riled

She is filled with impatience
   Blessed by a brother with patience
She is beautiful; hair of brown
   She is the new girl in town

Easter

Easter eggs; jelly beans & marshmallow chicks
    All bring a memory or two of spring
Baskets are filled with bunnies & grass
    Real grass is growing; hear the birds sing

Hats; new dresses; white gloves
    Fill all the churches to give worth
Family feasts & celebrations
    He rose from the dead; rebirth

New growth; new birth; new life
    Daffodils & tulips pop up in the yard
Puppies; kittens; new-born babies
    New life is unfolding; words from a bard

Rituals; sacrifices; pagan goddesses
    Symbols of a spring celebration with feist
Crosses; lambs & resurrection
    Symbols of Christianity; faith; Christ

Halloween

Halloween is celebrated on the last day in October
    It's also called "Hallows' Eve" or "All Saints' Eve"
It's a holiday that's celebrated all over the world
    A holiday that children should be guising, I believe

Pumpkins carved; turnips were carved in the past
    Costumes; Evil Spirits; make a ghost out of sheets
The origins of the holiday dates back to the Celts
    Story telling was done for tricks; for treats

Disguising, not guising, they hit the streets
    Action heroes replaced the rituals of the past
"Trick or Treat"; chanting that's done at each door
    Candy; safety; replaced perishables which last

This holiday is so commercial on American soil
    Best costume; decorations; the best product sold
All has forgotten to celebrate earth, harvest & spirit
    Now a time to be silly with no regard for the old

Will the spirits be angry, when no homage is paid?
    Will the harvest be fruitful, as seasons turns dark?
The celebration; centuries old; have we just forgotten?
    Careful; Mother-nature is waiting to make her mark

An American Holiday "Thanksgiving"

Thanksgiving is an "American" holiday, we believe
    It's the first feast in American Colony History
First feast of Pilgrims & Native Americans; to be
    Not officially called "Thanksgiving" until 1963

Thanksgiving is a celebration in November
    It has been given the 4th Thursday since 1863
The Civil war; Abraham Lincoln was the ember
    Declaring "Giving Thanks" day; celebrate with glee

The holiday; military victory or harvest celebration
    Give thanks & prayer; to share nature's wealth
A starting point for the holiday season; Exaltation!
    A day to give thanks for friends, family & health

We think of potatoes, gravy, yams & pumpkin pie
    A gathering of family, friends, children of all kind
Being thankful, depends on the person; that's no lie
    Some are just thankful for a meal; a place to unwind

Share a widow's mite! Help another not perish
    Share excess; Tis' the reason for the season
Reflect; make amends; a reminder for us to cherish
    This day of thanks is important for a reason

Christmas

Christmas is a magical time of the year
   Mistletoe; presents; Santa may appear
Christmas trees; Cookies; A hot toddy or two
   Stockings are hung; Presents for you

The hustle & bustle of this time of year
   Brings on stress & exhaustion; good cheer
What to buy, where to buy & what sale
   If we don't get the right thing, will we fail?

Christmas has become a commercial by far
   The money; the expense; could finance a car
Computers; I-phones; more money to spend
   No carols; hot cocoa; No hand to lend

Christmas has lost its true meaning I think
   As we buy more & more things that blink
We are supposed to celebrate Christ's birth
   Instead we publicize a red suit with girth

All can be if Christ is put back into Christmas
   If not, it's like taking "life" out of animas
Please dig deep; remember to put Christ back in
   Christmas is spiritual; don't make it a sin

Merry Christmas

Christmas comes but once a year
   From us to you, we send good cheer
We cherish you all year long
   But this is the time of year for song

"Silent Night" comes to mind
   The Christmas spirit you will find
"Away in a Manger" you'll listen with awe
   You see baby Jesus asleep in the straw

"Little Drummer Boy" tells the story that night
   They follow that single star so bright
"Oh Holy Night" tells of our Savior's birth
   Our Father's begotten son comes to earth

This poem is written by a Christmas mouse
   Because so much spirit is about our house
The song we've chosen for you with good cheer
   "Wish You a Merry Christmas & A Happy New Year!"

New Year

Our calendar is about to end
    What to do to start the New Year?
The winter solstice; some party; some pray
    Dancing; singing; drinking; Good cheer!

The "Ball" represents a New York new year
    The count down; people; Time Square
The "Peach" represents a Georgia new year
    In London, people gather in Trafalgar Square

Banging on doors; bamboo sticks & drums
    All rituals of old still practiced today
Noise; fireworks; food & more noise
    Still the process to ring in the first day

The old man; "Father Time" prepares to go
    Taking with him regrets & the past
The baby; birth of a new year ahead
    A new beginning; Resolution at last

Grab a noise maker & silly hat
    Raise the glass of sparkling wine
Let's get rid of the old; bring in the new
    Sing the song, "Auld Lang Syne"

The Color of My Skin

The color of my skin
    It should not matter
Whether I'm black or white
    Or clothes of tatter

The color of my skin
    It is a part of who I am
I could be smart, poor or rich
    There is no right to slam

The color of my skin
    Is only what you perceive
I am a human being; red blood
    The lord I shall receive

The color of my skin
    Doesn't make us all look the same
I am a different shape & shade
    This is my claim to fame

The color of my skin
    It is really only your dispute
What truly counts is inside
    If you can't be nice, please mute

Our Mother

As we look back at the pictures
    The ones of when she was so young
We can't see her as that person
    It was an era we did not walk among

Dresses & aprons; Hats with white gloves
    A lady was a lady & a man was a man
All roles were drawn & the manual set
    For each person to follow; quite a span

She became a wife & then a mother
    The pictures & person that we knew
Beautiful was her heart that she gave
    She gave it her best; we all grew

Times changed so much around her
    We, her children, grew up so fast
She instilled kindness, love & respect
    Part of who we are; woven; the bast

Cancer took her from this earth
    Grabbed her quick with no return
Too young to be taken; we still grieve
    For a hug; to this day, we all yearn

Mother

A female who is pregnant
   A woman who gives birth
This is a basic description
   Of one who nurtures on earth

There is no real definition
   The complexity has risen
The title can be social
   Cultural; or a mission

She is an inspiration of activity
   Like the mother of invention
This title "Mother" is sacred
   It needs much more attention

She is our source for hugs & safety
   One who cultivates our minds
She is a creative source of origin
   One who discovers or finds

She is someone who begets
   Or from whom we've learned
A title that is just given
   A title that should be earned

Marriage

Two people like each other
    They enjoy each other's company
They spend a lot of time together
    Where one goes, the other will accompany

Their hearts start to grow stronger
    They don't want to be apart
They're thoughts are about each other
    They are one in each other's heart

Thoughts of becoming married
    Thoughts of creating a home
Thoughts of creating a family
    All are answered in the biblical tome

Marriage is the joining of two lives
    It is sacred & should not be vogue
It is a contract that binds to lives
    It should not be done by a rogue

Vows are recited by two parties
    This changes both lives that enter
Whether religious, social, or jurisdiction
    It's a matter for the heart, not venter

Marriage, to enter one should be careful
    Entering should not be done for lust
Marriage should not be a controversial subject
    It is something to be proud of; A must

Sisters

Sisters are not just siblings
    Who share the same home
They are girls that are related
    Who speak the same gnome

They are biologically children
    From the same mom & dad
They are girls that are close
    Their blood; lineage clad

Their personalities can differ
    As does each birth order
It can depend on each other
    With or without disorder

Some say it is influence
    Some say it's their sign
Whether the girls get along
    Their lives inter-twine

True sisters just care
    True sisters are fun
They make each other happy
    Their lives cross as one

Think Positive

Think positive is what Mom & Dad used to say
   It brings positive electricity; negative not an ohm
Don't be negative; No-one wants negative around
   No matter what's in the world or close to home

Some think staying positive is just a waste of time
   Some know it's a mental attitude that expects good
A positive mind expects joy, happiness & kindness
   A subject undisputed. A subject time withstood

Staying positive can for sure change your life
   Being negative is a distraction; you lose focus
Some think that it's a book; CD; wave; or fad
   Being positive is mental power, you refocus

Inventors invent & overcome ups & downs
   If inventors were negative, would they get very far?
Being positive is a force that stays with you with use
   The more positive you become, the more you "Are"

I think I can; I think I can; an example for kids
   A positive tale for a person who shouldn't give up
There was no sad ending only happiness & success
   Proof that you can drink from that positive cup

Positive is as positive does; join the movement today
   Quickly jump on that spiritual wagon; if you would
You won't believe how natural the transformation
   Change in heart. Change, you too, should

A Conversation

Words are exchanged between two people
    Their meaning can be divine
The conversation can be short or long
    Exchanged over a glass of wine

The words may be said just in passing
    Depending on where you are at
The conversation can be quite musical
    If certain words are spoken in scat

The words may be said with some accent
    Depending on where people are from
The conversation can be emotional or not
    Exchanged with a hug or up thumb

The words can touch others without intent
    Their meaning differs for each mind
The conversation can be so touching
    If certain words are spoken as you unwind

The words might be meant to be said
    Depending on meaning or part of a path
The conversation may be meant to be
    Exchanged on purpose without wrath

The words are out there for all to use
    Depending on the education or exposure
The conversation can be so important to life
    If certain words are spoken for closure

Divorce

Divorce has become an American past time
   Right up there with baseball & apple pie
No one seems to stay together anymore
   Life together forever has become a big lie

You get this & I'll get that
   It becomes a "push comes to shove"
No one seems to remember the reasons
   As they wipe away the meaning of love

Divorce has come down to money & assets
   Instead of two hearts being torn
No one seems to remember the children
   As they become assets in the scorn

Divorce happens between mothers & fathers
   Main role models for our kids in herds
No one seems to take on the responsibility
   That all actions speak louder than words

There still is a few that honor the contract
   A few that stays together forever
There still is a few that "till death do us part"
   Means that they'll work on it & never sever

What happened to the staying together?
   What happened to the vow before God?
What happened to the contract that was signed?
   Has is just become an action considered mod?

Chocolate

A cacao bean tree is what is needed
   To make hot cocoa as sleek as mink
The Aztecs used the bean from the tree
   To make a bitter, restorative drink

Chocolate was given to only the worthy
   It was said that it induced much wisdom
When fermented this drink became powerful
   It was used for fertility in the kingdom

Chocolate has changed as centuries go by
   Chocolatiers have evolved, there are so many
Raspberry, orange, mint, dark or milk chocolate
   Dark is healthy but you can choose any

Chocolate is all around for your intake
   Its form comes in cookies, pasta, & bars
Some say it effects us psychologically
   It just feels good whether Hershey or Mars

Chocolate is eaten by more women than men
   It is good for your heart & your brain
The more you eat, the more you're smart
   A day without chocolate; how insane!

Chocolate has become a great gift for all
   It is something that never goes out of season
So give some chocolate & a smile to many
   It brings pleasure no matter the reason

Patience

Patience is a virtue; to be steadfast
   A state of endurance we're told
Having patience is a state of being
   From when we're young 'til we're old

Our lives have become such a bubble
   No longer caring about other's feelings
The end result does justify the means
   As we interact with each other; our dealings

Patience is something that is needed
   It is needed even more now
We live in such a fast paced world
   We've just lost the know how

We don't cherish or hold close values
   Our kids, our spouses, our mom & dad
Our lives have become self involved
   Something about this is just so sad

We all need less pride & more patience
   Be steadfast; endure; don't become an afrit
Patience is one of the greatest virtues of life
   It is one of the many fruits of the spirit

Tradition

Tradition is holding onto something significant
    It is how & what we want to pass down
It could be something from our family
    Or some celebration in our town

Participation helps hold onto memories
    It leaves part of us for the next who come
Without tradition, there is no history
    Of beliefs; customs, or practices for some

Traditions can be like some folklore
    The author or eldest is the holder
No one can dispute what is passed down
    If just one is left to speak; the molder

A tradition is like a family recipe
    Sometimes written or taught orally
But if things get out of hand; go astray
    It is changed; etiquette; to teach morally

Don't think that a tradition doesn't change
    The view is in the eyes of the beholder
To add something new or remove something bad
    It just makes the tradition somewhat bolder

Tradition establishes the legitimacy; the power
    To rebel is the act of treason; the effect
Tradition is for a group, to feel like they belong
    The basis behind what seems traditionally perfect

Autism

Autism is in families, neighborhoods & schools
   It is hard to diagnose; the causes not known
Many have theories & many place blame
   It is not from money, lineage or anything sewn

Autism is very difficult to diagnose
   There is not a biological test
Even doctors need special training
   To help mom & dad know what's best

They say it happens more in boys
   The exact number is not known
The causes are part of a list
   A list each one of us does own

Each of our babies is special & unique
   Each evolves & develops differently
Are we to blame if we allow individuality
   If we don't recognize with love intently

To help is to find out early
   To create a program or regimen
The specialists believe different theories
   So what to believe; when to begin

Don't forget that since there is no valid reason
   God has blessed each one with a special gift
Maybe poets, artists, & great entrepreneurs
   May have an unknown type of autism; time to shrift

Death

Death is final; death is the end
    You may never understand the loss
It takes a soul from loved ones on earth
    You lose so much more than dross

A father; a mother; a sibling; a child
    One that is part of your life as you live
The loss is huge as you continue to breathe
    Still so much more for them to give

Senescence is part of life as you know it
    The life of that person you so cherished
Pictures; Memories; Smiles; Jokes & songs
    Help keep a live memory of who has perished

Look into your own eyes & you will see
    Something that they have left for you
Your smile; your hair; your sister; your heart
    Look close, you'll recognize just a few

So hug your mom; your husband; your child
    They are your life now as you know it
You may miss the love of the one who has left
    Close your eyes; smile; remember the wit

Life

Life is so precious; life is so dear
    Don't waste a minute; don't spill
Stop; smell the roses; finish your list
    Don't waste a moment; get your fill

Each day in your life is so new
    Each day in your life is so fresh
Don't worry if today doesn't fit you
    Tomorrow everything will mesh

Walk slowly & breathe in happiness
    Quickly pass by & release your hurt
Forgiveness helps all who linger to long
    A true heart in life does not girt

Life is birth; life is growth; life is death
    You can choose each day or float through
The circle of time & life will continue
    Whether you take part or are stuck like glue

Dig deep; think hard as a free agent in charge
    Only you can start the process of dusting
Choose birth; choose growth; choose life
    Your attitude might need some adjusting

Lines for an Airplane Ride

It's funny how we all line up
   Multiple times before we ride
First the shuttle; train; or security line
   Then for a seat assignment, what side

Upon boarding the plane, we're in line again
   Only to wait for a seat that's assigned
Some like to settle quickly, others like to nest
   Only to move for others whom their aligned

Announcements are made before the door is shut
   Our finish line for last texts, emails, or calls
We all know how it works, yet we wait till the cut
   Another line item before the door handle falls

Seatbelts are a must no matter which seat we are in
   To be safe on take-off. We all know it's the law
We can't hear or ignore; the seatbelt sign yet again
   Attendant's walk the line to make sure they saw

It's time for a meal, beverage, or maybe a little snack
   How long in that line depends on where we were sat
First class has constant service & room to slack
   Coach is much different; No accommodation for fat

<u>(Continued on Next Page)</u>

Lines for an Airplane Ride (continued)

We wait again in line; the attendant collects trash
   The length of this line depends on workload
Impatient in line, we use the seat pocket to stash
   Irked; if we find that kind of trash down the road

Line after line: Yes another line as we deplane
   Depleting patience in each of the lines of our trek
We can't avoid airplane lines, unless we own a plane
   So online, not in line; another plane ticket; Heck!

In-Law

In-law is someone related by marriage
  Someone who is brought into the family
Sometimes they fit & sometimes they don't
  When the fit is right, all goes dandily

Each title in the family can be dashed by In-law
  It happens because of a contract of love
The title is a privilege; ends as a given right
  A title in which just appears hereinabove

This title is added to each member who joins
  A bloodline; new branch of the family tree
Money; Notoriety; may be part of this title
  It's a title that does not guarantee pedigree

Internet Dating

It happened so quick first a click then a chat
   Said yes to a lunch, a little worried it'd fail
Lunch was quite fun; laughed this & that
   Chat continued later with another e-mail

Hearts were open; tried to share
   Judged; then didn't give it a whirl
One's heart is true; to judge isn't fair
   Maybe that happens; an "Eastside" twirl

Tried; cared; One wished it was real
   Choice "to be" came with, "What rule"
Was honest; up front; felt like a good deal
   Rules ruined the deal; looked like a fool

No call; No show; what to think?
   Was one hurt? Did one care at all?
Worried; wanted closure; was gone in a wink
   The actions, not right, that's definitely all

Forgave & gave up; Yes, "Oh my, my!"
   Was it real? A prowler or maybe a bet
Actions, no accountancy; so abrupt, "Bye, Bye
   "Quality"; definitely not found with that net

If You "Are" What You Eat

If you "Are" what you eat
   I'm a chicken croquette
I can't see myself as pig's feet
   Please hold off on my "Are" title just yet

Is the "Are" title per day, meal, or holiday?
   Can't imagine being held to one "Are" choice or meal
For breakfast I'd know what my "Are" would say
   I'm bacon, eggs, toast, & home fries, for real

The "Are" title can't possibly be a stagnant state
   My food choices are eclectic thus far
My belly, for sure, could not pass or wait
   For the "Are" title to change for a cookie bar

My "Are" title is like an electronic picture frame
   It changes with my entire intake
Pumpkin pie; Chocolate Éclairs; No shame
   My "Are" title should be sweet, not fake, with flake

About the Author

My name is Dolly M. Gorham. I am one of 5 children. I am the daughter of Charles Kenneth Gorham & Margaret Leah (Hawley) Gorham. Both parents were born in the early 1920's. They grew up during the depression experiencing & watching so many changes in America. Their knowledge, history, & influence are a big part of who I am.

I grew up in Lancaster, Massachusetts. The town of Lancaster is rich with old architecture as it was founded in the early 1600's. The countryside was rich in poetic history. Emily Dickinson, Ralph Waldo Emerson, Henry David Thoreau & Robert Frost all walked, wrote, & lived around where I grew up. My biggest influence came from Robert Frost.

I feel that my poetry is plain & simple. My subjects are about basic America. I have had many people read my poetry & they urged me to compile my writing in order to publish. As they shared their thoughts after reading, I gained enough confidence to pursue this book.

I am a member of the Academy of American Poets.

Notes:

Notes:

Notes:

Notes:

Notes:

Notes:

Notes:

Notes:

Notes: